FIRST STEPS IN THE LOVE OF GOD

Drawn from the Writings of
St Francis de Sales

All booklets are published thanks to the generous support of the members of the Catholic Truth Society

CATHOLIC TRUTH SOCIETY
PUBLISHERS TO THE HOLY SEE

Contents

Introduction 3

Love and Salvation 4
The Love of God and Human Nature 7
The Love of God the Means of Salvation 9
The Love of God has dominion over all other loves 11
The Love of God and God's Grace 13
The Sweetness of Love's Attraction 14
The Love of God and Penitence 19

The Life of Love 23
God desires that we should increase in His Love 23
God has made His Love so easy 27
Perseverance in the Love of God 29
The Love of God and Death 32
Our Blessed Lady's Love of God 35
The Love of God and Humility 37

INTRODUCTION

Francis de Sales was born near Annecy in 1567. He was consecrated to the See of Geneva in 1602, and became one of the very great Bishops in the history of the Church. But his first mission as a young priest had been to win back to the Catholic faith the people of his native Chablais, who had almost all gone over to Calvinism. His dramatic success was partly due to his discovery of a powerful new weapon of evangelisation: the pamphlet. Every week Francis wrote and distributed leaflets explaining the Catholic faith in simple and direct language. After four years, the people of the Chablais had returned to the practice of their ancient religion.

This pamphlet first appeared in the series The People's Manuals brought out by Cardinal Vaughan.

It is taken chiefly from the first books of the classic Treatise on the Love of God by St Francis de Sales.

Needless to say, large portions of the Saint's work are entirely omitted: philosophical and technical disquisitions have been passed over, and whole chapters have been condensed. But the pamphlet, though presented in its own form, contains the thought and teaching of St Francis de Sales, and, for the most part, in the words of the Saint.

LOVE AND SALVATION

"You must love the Lord your God with all your heart, with all your soul, and with all your mind. This is the greatest and the first commandment" (Matt.23,37-38). I sought you outside myself, but I found you not, because you are within me.

Faith shows us that God is, that He is infinite in goodness, that He can communicate Himself to us; not only that He can, but that He will. The human heart is troubled with unsatisfied desires and continual uneasiness; it longs for perfect satisfaction and solid contentment. It tends naturally towards God without knowing what He is, but when it finds Him by Faith and sees Him so good, so lovely, so gracious, so ready to give Himself to all who desire Him, it is filled with delight because it realizes that it has found that which it desires and can be at rest. The human heart, by a deep and secret instinct in all its actions, aims at felicity, seeking it here and there without knowing where it is to be found or in what it consists, till Faith shows it that in God only can it rest. Before, it knew not what to aim at: nothing contented it because it did not know what it wanted; it was seeking to love and knew not what to love; it was seeking God and knew not where to find Him, and though it had sufficient foretaste of love to make it seek, it had not sufficient knowledge of the goodness of God to make it love or to make it practise love.

When we concentrate our thoughts on God, our hearts are stirred by various emotions, and our understanding is filled with a certain pleasure in the very thought of the Divinity, the smallest knowledge of which is worth more than the greatest knowledge of all other things. When misfortune befalls us we have recourse to God because when all fails us we feel that He alone can befriend us, and when we are in peril He alone, as our Protector, can save and succour us. This confidence which the human heart has in God proves that there exists an affinity between His divine goodness and our soul, a great but a secret affinity which cannot be denied, of which everyone is more or less conscious, but of which few think, and which no one really understands. We know that we are created to His image and likeness, and what does this mean but that there exists a connection between God and the Soul?

But, besides this affinity of likeness between God and the Soul, there is a bond of union between God and Man for their reciprocal perfection: not that God can receive any perfection from man, but as man cannot be perfected but by God, so God never bestows His graces outside Himself more perfectly than when He bestows them on humanity; the one being needy and capable of receiving, the other possessing all things with the desire of giving.

Therefore God had greater pleasure in bestowing His graces on us than we have in receiving them from Him.

The spouse of The Song of Songs desiring the holy kiss of union says, "Let him kiss me with the kisses of his mouth" (Sg.1,2). She aspires and implores to be united to Him whom she loves, "Your love is more delightful than wine; delicate is the fragrance of your perfume" (Sg.1,2-3).

New wine boils and bubbles and cannot contain itself within the casks because of its strength and goodness, but "your love is 'more' delightful than wine": it attracts us more powerfully. Your love presses and urges us to love You, and, to draw the children of Your heart into Your love, it sends forth a fragrance which is sweeter than the choicest perfume.

The void in our hearts can only be filled by God. The emptiness of the human heart desires God's gracious gifts, for we are poor and needy, but God who possesses riches in abundance has no need of our poverty. The excellence of His divine perfections cannot be enhanced or increased by communication, for He acquires nothing in the outpouring of Himself, being the source of all grace and the inexhaustible fountain of grace. The more He gives, the more He has to give; but our poverty would remain wanting and miserable were it not enriched by the graces He bestows with such magnificent liberality. The soul, once it has realised the vanity of all earthly things, sees by the light of Faith that to attain the happiness it seeks, it must unite itself to the divine goodness who alone can satisfy all its desires.

The Love of God, and Human Nature

Although our nature is depraved by sin, an inclination to love God remains in the soul, and the light by which we see His sovereign goodness to be so worthy of our love exists there also. This makes it impossible to think of God attentively without feeling a certain amount of love, which being excited stirs our hearts to love God as He only deserves to be loved. Moreover, though we are formed, bred, and nourished in the midst of material, base, and transitory things, tied down as it were by the strings of nature, yet at the first look our soul casts on God, at its first knowledge of Him, the inclination to love, which was dull and imperceptible at first, awakes, and suddenly appears as a spark among ashes, making us desire to love Him with the love which is due to the sovereign and first principle of all things.

But we have not of ourselves the power to love God above all things, though we may have the desire to do so. Eagles have great hearts and much strength of wing, but we are told that they can see farther than they can fly. So the soul animated by a holy desire towards the Divinity has more light in the understanding to see how loveable God is, than force in the will to love Him. Sin has weakened man's will far more than it has darkened his intellect, and though the rebellion of the sensual appetite which we call concupiscence disturbs the understanding, it is against the will that it stirs up sedition and revolt. Thus the will, already weak, is so shaken by the continual assaults which are directed against it by concupiscence, that it cannot make the progress in divine love which reason and inclination would desire. Our wretched nature spoilt by sin is like the palm tree, which in a cold clime bears but imperfect fruit and requires heat in order to produce ripe and seasoned dates. In like manner our hearts may produce imperfect beginnings of God's love, but to love Him with a perfect love that is above all things, belongs only to hearts assisted by grace and inflamed by holy charity.

The little imperfect love which in the beginning of our conversion stirs our hearts is a weak will, a will that would but wills not, a sterile will which does not produce true effects. It is a will sick of the palsy which sees the beautiful pond of holy love, but which has neither the strength nor the generosity to love God above all things. The Apostle, speaking in the person of the sinner, says, "The fact is, I know of nothing good living in me - living, that is, in my unspiritual self - for though the will to do what is good is in me, the performance is not" (Rom.7,18).

Ah! how good God has been to us: He has imprinted on our nature the light of His divine countenance, and given joy to our hearts in giving them an inclination to love Him. More than this, He has given us a thirst for the precious waters of His love, and though we cannot of ourselves love Him with that love which is due to Him, He has promised that He will conduct us in all sweetness till He has brought us to this sovereign love for which He has created us.

Hence the Royal Prophet calls this inclination of the human heart towards God, not only a light - in that it makes us see where we are inclined - but also a joy or gladness, for it comforts us when we stray, giving us hope that God who has engraved and left in us this clear mark of our origin, intends and desires to bring us back to Himself if we will but throw ourselves into the arms of His infinite goodness.

The Love of God the Means of Salvation

Although our Saviour's redemption is applied to our souls in many and different ways, love is the universal means of salvation which mingles with everything and without which nothing is profitable. The cherubim were placed at the gate of the earthly paradise with flaming sword to teach us that no one shall enter the heavenly paradise who is not pierced through with the sword of love. Our Lord who bought us with His Blood is infinitely desirous that we should love Him that we may be saved, and desires our salvation that we may love Him eternally. "I have come to bring fire to the earth, and how

I wish it were blazing already" (Luke 12,49). In order to show us the ardour of His desire and what kind of love He requires of us, He tells us "You must love the Lord your God with *all* your heart, with *all* your soul, and with *all* your mind. This is the greatest and the first commandment" (Matt.22,37-38).

How amorous the divine Heart is of our love! God does not merely give us a permission to love Him, as Laban permitted Jacob to love his fair Rachel and to earn her by service, but He makes a passionate declaration of His love for us and commands us to love Him with our whole heart, lest the thought of His Divine Majesty on the one hand and our misery on the other might alarm us from His love. In this He shows us that the desire to love which He puts into our hearts is not planted there for nothing, for He urges us by a commandment to use it and not to leave it idle, and He gives to all abundant means of putting this command into practice.

As the sun touches and heats the earth with its vivifying rays giving to all things, even the most inferior, strength and vigour to increase and produce, so God animates all souls and encourages all hearts to love Him. None are excluded from the heat of His love: all have the means of obtaining this love. "Our sins and crimes weigh heavily on us; we are wasting away because of them. How are we to go on living?" Say to them, "As I live - it is the Lord Yahweh who speaks - I take pleasure, not in the death of a wicked man, but in the turning back of a wicked man who changes his ways to win life" (Ezk.33,10-11).

Now to live according to God is to love, for "If you refuse to love, you must remain dead" (1 Jn.3,15). See how much God desires that we should love Him!

The Love of God has dominion over all other loves

The will governs all the faculties, but she is in turn governed by love which makes her desire to be like that which she loves. Now of all loves the love of God is the noblest. It holds the sceptre, and has authority so inseparably united to and proper to its nature that if it be not master, it ceases to be and perishes. Divine love takes up its abode in the higher regions of the soul, where it offers sacrifice and holocausts to the Divinity as Abraham did. Our Saviour sacrificed Himself on Mount Calvary that from the mountain top His commandment to love might be heard and obeyed by His people. Those who obey His commands - the souls who with all their faculties and affections give themselves up to His love - He governs with ineffable sweetness. Love has not convicts or slaves, but brings all under her sway with a force sweet and delicious, for nothing is so strong as love, and nothing is so sweet as love's strength. God wills that as in Himself so in man all things should be ordered by love and for love. "I have loved you with an everlasting love, so I am constant in my affection for you" (Jr.31,3).

Our Lord is not content with a public declaration of His desire to be loved, so that all may share in His sweet invitation, but He goes from door to door knocking and protesting, "Look, I am standing at the door, knocking. If one of you hears me calling and opens the door, I will come in to share his meal, side by side with him" (Rv.3,20). That is, He will give all good things, graces which lead us to prayer and penance, a rich ample sufficiency of grace to love Him above all things, which He freely bestows on us sinners with royal magnificence such as is to be expected from so great a King.

Behold this divine Lover at the gate: He not only knocks, but He *stands* knocking at the door of our heart. He calls the soul, "Come then, my love, my lovely one, come" (Sg.2,10). He puts His hand into the lock to try if He cannot open it. If He utters His voice in the streets, He does not simply utter it, but He goes crying out, calling us to penance, asking us for our love. He forgets nothing to show us that His mercies are above all His works, that His mercy surpasses His judgments, that His redemption is copious and His love infinite in order to gain our hearts and to reclaim us from our misery. If by disloyalty we have abandoned Him, His compassion is excited and He sends us the gentle wind of His holy inspirations, which, blowing on our hearts, heats them, raising our thoughts and moving our affections into the atmosphere of divine Love.

The Love of God and God's Grace

If we received divine inspirations to the full extent of their virtue we should make great progress in sanctity. The Holy Spirit, like a spring of living water, flows into every part of our heart spreading His graces, but He will not enter without the consent of our free will, and He will only pour forth grace according to His good pleasure and according to our disposition and co-operation. St Paul exhorts us "not to neglect the grace of God that you have received" (2 Co.6,1). We receive the grace of God in vain, when we receive it at the door of our heart and not with the consent of our will. It is useless to *feel* divine inspiration without consenting to it. When God moves us to embrace His holy love, if we do not consent with our *whole* heart it will profit us but little; if being moved to do much for God we only consent to do a little we resemble the people in the Gospel who when Our Lord bade them follow Him made reservations, one to go and bury his father, the other to go and take leave of his people. God bids us ask Him to enlarge our poor hearts, and when we allow Him to dilate them, He pours forth a ceaseless stream of divine grace into our souls which makes us increase in heavenly love. If we refuse our consent, He stops because we do not correspond to his inspirations.

St Francis of Assisi was once asked what opinion he had of himself. The saint answered, "I believe myself to be the greatest sinner in the world and one who serves Our Lord least". His companion asked him how he could hold such an opinion of himself truthfully, seeing what great sins were committed by others. St Francis answered, "If God had favoured the sinners of whom you speak as He has favoured me, I am certain that they would have acknowledged God's gifts far better than I do, and would serve Him far better than I do, and if my God abandoned me I should be more wicked than anyone".

Though it was humility which made St Francis speak thus of himself, he knew that an equal grace might be more faithfully employed by one sinner than by another, and if this was the opinion of the Seraphic Saint, St Bonaventure, the great doctor of the science of the saints who learnt his lesson of love at the foot of the Crucifix, it shows us how careful we should be to correspond most faithfully to the grace of God, "who wants everyone to be saved and reach full knowledge of the truth (1 Tm.2,4).

The Sweetness of Love's Attraction

We do not speak here of those miraculous graces which are almost instantaneous in their effect and which have suddenly transformed wolves into lambs, rocks into water, persecutors into preachers. We leave on one side those holy and violent attractions by which God brings some souls from the extremity of vice to the extremity of grace, such as were given to Saul, who became Paul the "chosen instrument" (Acts 9,15). Generally speaking, God converts souls so gently and delicately that His action is hardly perceptible; "I led them with reins of kindness, with leading-strings of love" (Ho.11,4). We are not drawn to God by iron chains, but by attractions and holy inspirations, which are the cords of Adam and adapted to our human hearts. The band of the human will is delight and pleasure. We show nuts to a child, says St Augustine, and he is drawn by love; he is drawn by the cords not of his body but of his heart.

Observe how tenderly the Eternal Father deals with His children. While He teaches us He delights us. He does not force us. He casts into our hearts spiritual pleasures as sacred baits in order to draw us, making us taste the sweetness of His doctrine, and though God teaches and surrounds the soul with innumerable inspirations, invitations, and attractions, He leaves it perfectly free. Grace is so gracious that she does not constrain or interfere with the liberty of our free will; grace touches powerfully, yet so delicately that our free will suffers no violence. Grace has power not to force but to attract the heart. Grace presses us but does not compel us; so that under the action of her power we can consent or resist as we wish. But when our will follows the attraction and consents to the divine action, she follows freely as she resists freely; and though the consent to grace depends more on grace than on the will, the resistance to grace depends on the will only. So sweetly and delicately does God deal with each individual soul. Our Lord said to the Samaritan woman, "If you only knew what God is offering *and who it is that* is saying to you: 'Give me a drink', you would have been the one to ask, and he would have given you living water" (Jn.4,10).

Mark Our Lord's way of speaking of His attractions.

"If you only knew what God is offering" you would without doubt be moved and attracted to ask for "the water of eternal life", and *perhaps* you would ask for it, as though He said "you would have power and be provoked to ask it, yet not forced to do so", but only "perhaps you would have asked", for you are free to ask or not to ask; and when we say we have the power to reject divine inspirations, we do not mean we can hinder God from inspiring us or touching our hearts, for that is done by God - in us yet without us. "No one can come to me unless he is drawn by the Father" (Jn.6,44).

God set us in motion, but if we refuse to move we resist. Now when God offers to carry us into the atmosphere of holy love, our will is moved by the delectation we feel, and if we consent to the action of God's grace, ah! how happy we are, for God will help us, conducting and accompanying us from love to love till we enter the Land of Promise.

LOVE AND SALVATION

What joy, what consolation it is to consider the secret method by which the Holy Spirit pours the first rays of His light and heat into our hearts. Oh, Jesus! what joy to contemplate celestial love, this sun of justice, as by degrees and almost insensibly it enlightens the soul, drawing it till it reaches the perfect beauty of love's day. How beautiful, how glorious this daybreak is, although the break of day is not the perfect day itself, for at first our love is but an imperfect love. The soul is beginning only to put forth the buds of love, which, when warmed by the sun of love, will blossom into the fruits of love, if we be but faithful to God's grace.

Pachonius, a young infidel soldier, came with his troops to a village near Thebes, where he found no food. The inhabitants of the village were Christians and forthwith supplied all his wants. Pachonius asked to what nation they belonged, and he was told that they were Christians, that they believed in Jesus Christ the only Son of God, and did good to all because they knew that God would reward them. Now Pachonius was naturally of a noble character though he was asleep in infidelity until God, by the example of the Christians, showed him that the Christian law was a law of love. Pachonius accepted the first grace of God offered him, for he studied the doctrine of our Saviour, and his soul was filled with light and consolation. Entering into himself he lifted up his hands towards heaven and said, "Lord God, who has made heaven and earth, if you deign to cast your eyes on my misery and baseness and to give me knowledge of your Divinity, I promise to serve You and to obey Your commandments all the days of my life". After this prayer and promise, the love of God increased in him, and he practised many acts of virtue during the remainder of his life. The grace of God had touched his heart, filling it with spiritual sweetness, and Pachonius corresponded to the grace God offered him, and placing his whole confidence in God he breathed forth a humble and loving prayer, in which he begged for a more perfect knowledge of God, that he might serve Him perfectly.

God touches our hearts very gently, strengthening them by degrees till He obtains from us our full consent. Then He draws us unto Himself step by step. "Draw me in your footsteps" says the sacred spouse, "let us run" (Sg.1,4) that is, You begin first - I cannot move of myself - but You move me, and once You have set me in motion, then, O Spouse of my heart, "we will run". You go before me drawing me ever forward. I will follow You and consent to Your drawing. Let no one think You drag me like a forced slave. Ah, no! You draw me by the fragrance of your perfume. Your drawing is mighty but not violent. Its whole force lies in its sweetness, like perfumes which have no power other than their sweetness - and how can the sweetness of the love of God draw the soul, unless deliciously?

The Love of God and Penitence

Perfect penitence springs from love and is mingled with love. St Paul says: "If I give away all that I possess, piece by piece, and if I even let them take my body to burn it, but am without love, it will do me no good whatever" (1 Cor.13,3). Were our penitence so great as to cause our eyes to melt away in tears and our hearts to break with sorrow, if we have no love of God it would profit us nothing for eternal life. With remorse and sorrow for sin God often puts into our hearts the sacred fire of His love; this love is converted into tears, and by a second change our tears are converted into a greater fire of love. Mary Magdalen when she saw Our Lord wept. Her tears, which flowed from the sorrow she felt for her sins, made her love Him more ardently, and the Gospel tells us that many sins were forgiven her because "she loved much".

The loving consideration of God's infinite goodness to us who have offended Him by sin produces the waters of holy penitence, and from these waters issues the fire of divine love. Perfect penitence reconciles and reunites us to God in the quality of love, and through this love our tears become tears of joy and our sorrow is changed into consolation. Mary Magdalen sought her Lord saying "They have taken my Lord away and I don't know where they have put him" (Jn.20,13), but when through sorrow and sighs and tears she finds Him, she holds Him and keeps Him by love. Imperfect love desires and runs after Him, penitence seek and finds Him: perfect love holds and clasps Him, for love steeped in the bitterness of penance gains strength and becomes excellent love.

The infinite goodness of God being the motive of perfect repentance, and the love of God making our contrition more perfect, urge us to pray for the great grace of His love. We may pray thus "I am Yours, save me. Have mercy on me, O God, have mercy on me: for my soul trusts in You. Save me, O God, for the waters have come even into my soul. Make me as one of Your hired servants. O God, be merciful to me a sinner".

Humble and contrite prayer raises up the soul to God, re-uniting it to His infinite goodness; it obtains pardon by the love from which it springs and therefore we ought frequently to use such ejaculatory prayers, humbly seeking to be reconciled to God and laying our tribulations at our Saviour's feet, pouring ourselves out before Him, hiding ourselves in His precious Wounds and bathing our souls in the precious Blood; entering even into His sacred Heart which is open to all, and which receives sinners with such tender mercy.

To conclude, we have seen how God, by a progress full of sweetness, conducts the soul which He draws out of the Egypt of sin, from love to love, till He has brought her to the land of promise, that is, holy charity. This is a friendship and a disinterested love, for by charity we love

God for His own sake, and because of His infinite goodness we desire to be united to Him by love. He fosters our desire to love Him and never ceases to speak to our hearts by inspirations and allurements, giving us all manner of proof of His love for us, revealing to us His secrets as to His most confidential friends. To crown His loving intercourse with us He makes Himself our proper food in the most Holy Sacrament of the Eucharist, where He remains in our midst that we may speak with Him at all times in holy prayer. Now, this friendship is not an ordinary friendship, but a friendship of dilection, by which we choose God in order to love Him with a special love. He is chosen, says the sacred spouse, "among ten thousand" (Sg.5,10). She says, "among ten thousand", but she means out of all.

Charity loves God above all things, and this love is raised far above all earthly affection, so that other loves are not true loves in comparison to the love of God, or, if earthly love be true love, the love of God is infinitely more than love, and, therefore, it is not a love which the force of nature, either angelic or human, can produce. The Holy Spirit gives it - "because the love of God has been poured into our hearts by the Holy Spirit" (Rm.5,5). Charity, then, is a love of friendship, a friendship of dilection, a dilection of preference, a preference incomparable, sovereign, and supernatural. Like a sun, it enlightens the soul, perfecting all the spiritual faculties, for, seated in the will as on its throne, there it reigns, making the heart cherish and love its God above all things. Oh, how happy is the soul wherein this holy love is poured, because "all good things came to me" (Ws.7,11).

THE LIFE OF LOVE

"Let those who do good go on doing good, and those who are holy continue to be holy" (Rv.22,11)

God desires that we should increase in His Love

"The path of the virtuous is like the light of dawn, its brightness growing to the fullness of day" (Pr.4,18). The Council of Trent assures us that the friends of God, proceeding from virtue to virtue, are day by day renewed, that is, they increase by good works in the justice which they receive by God's grace, and are more and more justified. St Paul says: "My prayer is that your love for each other may increase more and more and never stop improving your knowledge and deepening your perception" (Ph.1,9). To remain at a standstill in the love of God is impossible: he that gains not, loses in the exercise of love; he that ascends not, descends the ladder; he that vanquishes not in the battle, is vanquished.

Our life on earth is a perpetual warfare which our enemies wage against us, if we do not resist we perish, and we do not resist unless we overcome ourselves, but, when we overcome, we triumph. It is written of man that he "blossoms, and he withers, like a flower, fleeting as a shadow, transient" (Jb.14,2). He either goes forward or backwards, "All the runners at the stadium are trying to win, but only one of them gets the prize" (1 Cor.9,24). Who is the prize but Jesus Christ? and how can we take hold of Him unless we follow Him? and if we follow Him, we shall run continually, for He never stayed, but continued His course of love and obedience until death, even until the death of the cross. Those who go with Our Lord walk in the path of love, and their love for Him admits of no other bounds but those of life, and as long as life remains, they run after this loving Saviour. They run *ardently* and *swiftly,* knowing that there is nothing better than to follow Him, even if they be not so happy as to take hold of Him.

"I have inclined my heart to do Your justifications forever", says the Prophet. He does not say for a time, but forever, and because he desires eternally to do well, he shall have an eternal reward. "Happy all those who fear Yahweh and follow in His paths" (Ps.128,1). In this life we are on the way, and the way is made not to *rest* in, but to *go* in, and God speaking to one of His servants, says: "Bear yourself blameless in my presence" (Gn.17,1).

True love has no limits, it goes ever further, and holy charity, which is the virtue of virtues, having an infinite object, would be capable of becoming infinite if it could meet with a heart capable of infinity. Nothing hinders love from being infinite excepting the condition of the will which receives it and which acts by it; a condition which prevents us from seeing Him as much as He is visible. The heart which could love God with a love equal to the divine goodness would have a will infinitely good, which cannot be but in God.

Charity may be perfected in us up to the infinite, that is, charity may increase in us, it may become more and more excellent, but never infinite. The Holy Spirit may elevate our hearts and apply them to what supernatural actions He pleases, so they be not infinite. Indeed our soul is highly honoured in that it is in this mortal life. Moreover God has made the increase of His love so easy; the cup of cold water given for the love of God has its reward; according to human judgment it is but a small matter hardly worthy of consideration, but God judges it otherwise, and recompenses it.

All our little actions performed from love are pleasing to God, and are meritorious. It is said that in Arabia all plants are sweet, even those which are not of themselves odoriferous, and this because of the perfume of the soil in which they grow. So in the loving soul, her smallest actions, being performed from love and springing from love, have a good odour before the Majesty of God, who forthwith gives her an increase of charity. Our Holy Mother the Church, in teaching us to pray, says, "O Lord, give us the increase of faith, hope, and charity", and St Paul assures us that "there is no limit to the blessings which God can send you" (2

Cor.9,8) and God gives us this increase according to the use we made of His grace.

"For anyone who has" which means, whoever uses the favours he receives well, "will be given more and he will have more than enough", (Matt.13,12) and Our Lord tells us to lay up for ourselves treasures in heaven (Matt.6,20) ever to add new good works to the former ones, for prayer, fasting, and almsdeeds are the coins whereof our treasures are to consist.

Among the treasures of the Temple, the poor widow's mite was much esteemed, and as by the addition of many little pieces of coin the whole treasure increases in value, so our little works, even when they are performed somewhat coldly, are agreeable to God. His goodness is such that He values all we give Him, and He rewards us with an increase of charity here and assigns to us a greater degree of heavenly glory hereafter. A heart inflamed with divine love endeavours to bring forth works full of fervour, so that its love of God may be greatly increased; yet if we will only give to God works of lesser value, we shall not lose our reward, for God is pleased by these, that is, He will love us a little more for them.

Now God never loves a soul more without bestowing upon her more charity, our love for Him being the proper and special effect of His love for us.

God has made His Love so easy

"Yes, my yoke is easy and my burden light" (Matt.11,30). God makes all things easy to those who give themselves up to His love, and when He draws a soul and shows her that He intends her to walk in the path of perfection, He does not ask her to do so alone. He goes with her, urging her to go forward in the path of love, and showing her how to make good use of the love which He Himself has put into her heart. "While we have the chance, we must do good to all" (Gal.6,10).

When God condescends to cast His gracious eyes on the soul, she should humbly fix her whole attention on the divine Goodness, who thus honours her with His love, answering every invitation He makes her, giving Him great and fervent works of love, and small and lowly works full of love. God loves each one of us so ardently that His desire is to make us increase in the love we owe Him. He makes all things easy; He renders all things profitable to us, and turns all our endeavours, be they ever so feeble, to our gain. Nor is this strange, for the love of God is the noblest of all love. It has nothing great or small which is not loveable; it is all holy, and it brings forth nothing that is not worthy of love, or does not tend to love.

The soul is the spouse of Christ when she is just. She is just when she is in charity, and she is no sooner spouse than she is led into the cabinet of delicious perfumes mentioned in the Song of Songs. Now when a soul thus honoured commits sin, she ceases to look on her spouse in order to enjoy the vanities of earthly things, but when she realises her folly she is stung by remorse of conscience, and she returns to her spouse enamoured. He fortifies her, and conducts her through faith, hope, and penitence, till He restores her to spiritual health, which is no other thing but charity. In her trials He supports and sustains her, and it is hard to say whether she goes, or whether she is carried in the arms of her Beloved. I walk, "or rather the grace of God that is with me" (1 Cor.15,10). Thus she renders glory to God, and acknowledges that she lives, walks, and works in Him, and by Him.

Though we walk in the presence of God, and make progress in His love, it is the goodness of God which ever helps the soul to whom He has given His love, for He continually holds her with His holy hand. In doing so He shows her the sweetness of His love for her, He animates her more and more, He supports her against evil inclinations and habits contracted by former sins, and He strengthens her against temptations.

God desires that we should advance in the way of perfection, and He urges us and solicits us to make good use of the grace of love which he gives us. And though charity, however weak, enables us to perform the works necessary for salvation, to aspire to a great love of God, to undertake great works for God, our hearts need to be

Our Lord continually helps and conducts His children, making them walk before Him, giving them His hand in difficulties, and sometimes even taking them into His arms Those who love God fear no evil, for they have a firm and childlike confidence in Him. They trust Him implicitly, for they know that He will accomplish in them the work of salvation which He begins, "Who puts both the will and the action into you" (Phil.2,13).

The souls who really love God ardently desire to persevere in the love of God to the end. No one can persevere who does not pray. "The love of Christ overwhelms us" (2 Cor. 5:14). Those who love press Our Lord to increase their love, and press Him to give them perseverance in His love, begging Him to remain with them, as did the disciples in Emmaus, who not only petitioned Our Lord, but pressed - forcibly urged Him - compelled Him by a loving violence to remain in the lodging with them. "Yes, Lord, I am Yours, all Yours without reserve. Ah, Lord, draw me still deeper into Your heart for I am weak; make me persevere in Your love to the end - that Your love may draw me - that I may be swallowed up in its sweetness".

Prayer is the only means of obtaining love and perseverance in love, for we are so weak that we can do nothing of ourselves. Humble and persevering prayer obtains everything. Prayer is to go to God for everything. Some go to Him to hear Him as did Mary Magdalen, some inflamed with love, to be raised by the hand of this heavenly lover.

The saints could never have done such great and generous things for God, unless God had increased the love which they had in their hearts, and given them special inspirations, invitations, lights, and graces, by which He urged and helped them to perform wonderful exploits of spiritual valour.

The young man in the Gospel whom Our Lord loved, and who consequently was in charity, never dreamt of selling all he had and of giving it to the poor, and of following his Saviour, until Our Lord gave him the inspiration, and even then he had not the courage to put it into execution. Holy Church makes us pray thus: "Move our hearts, O Lord. Guide our actions by Your holy inspirations and further them with Your continual help. O Lord, make haste to help us" that by such prayers we may obtain grace to perform great works of love, and frequently and fervently to do smaller works full of love, and that we may have grace to overcome our evil inclinations and strength to resist all temptation.

Perseverance in the Love of God

"I am Yahweh, your God... and I love you. Do not be afraid, for I am with you" (Is.43,3-5). As a tender mother assists and supports her babe, letting it sometimes venture a step by itself, at other times carrying it in her arms, so to be cured by Him, as the woman who had the issue of blood; others to adore Him as the three kings, others to serve Him as Martha, others to overcome their unbelief as Thomas; some to embalm Him as Joseph of Arimathea, some to get the better of their fear and cowardice as Nicodemus; others seek Him - and find Him - and when they have found Him they remain with Him as the Sulamitess who holds Him and desires never to quit Him; never to quit Him is to persevere in our love for Him, and to persevere to the end. "I held Him fast, nor would I let Him go" (Sg.3,4).

The love of God is the union of the soul to God by love, and the perfection of this union consists in its being pure, in its being strong, in its being stable or persevering. "No one can come to me unless he is drawn by the Father who sent me" (Jn.6,44). The soul who desires to be united to God prays that she may love - prays that she may persevere in love.

Our perfect model in love, in prayer, in perseverance, and in sacrifice, is Our Blessed Lady at the foot of her Son's Cross. "What do you seek, O Mother, on this Mount of Calvary, in this place of death?" She seeks Him who is the Life of her life. Why did she seek Him? To be near Him, for it was not joy she sought, but her crucified Love, and her heart full of love made her seek *always* to be united to Him whom she loved.

"The man who stands firm to the end will be saved" (Matt.10,22). The love of God is the most precious gift we can hope for in this life, and for perseverance in this love we must pray. We cannot have it but from the hand of God, who alone can assure him who stands, and help him who falls. Therefore, we must incessantly ask for it, making use of the means Our Lord has taught us, which are prayer, fasting, and almsdeeds, frequenting the sacraments, intercourse with the good, and reading and hearing holy words. The gift of perseverance is granted to all who ask it and who give their full consent to the graces God offers them. Consequently, it is in our power to persevere, and, if we pray, we may all say with the Apostle that "neither death nor life, no angel, no prince, nothing that exists, nothing still to come, not any power, or height or depth, nor any created thing, can ever come between us and the love of God made visible in Christ Jesus our Lord" (Rom.8,38-9).

The Love of God and Death

"O grave, where is your victory? O death, where is your sting?"

The perfect union of the soul with God can only be in heaven, when the labours and dangers of this mortal life are over and the soul arrives at the gate of the heavenly Jerusalem, where she will behold the King of Glory seated on His throne.

THE LIFE OF LOVE

The soul who loves God desires with a holy ardour to be united to God, to be absorbed in Him, and though she is satisfied to remain on earth as long as He wills her to do so, she knows that her thirst for her God cannot be slaked until her Spouse gives her to drink of the waters of eternal life.

The heavenly Kings strengthens the soul who has given herself up to His love during life, and He assists her at the hour of her death - the longed for hour when she will be united to her Spouse in eternal glory, when she will receive the reward of holy perseverance, for she has desired "to be gone and be with Christ" (Phil.1,23).

Ravished with the love of her Well-beloved, she recalls the multitude of favours and graces which her God gave her while she was on her pilgrimage. She kisses the sweet and holy hand of God which drew her, conducted, and supported her on her way, and she confesses that all she is and all she has she holds from her divine Lord and Master - all are the gifts of His love.

O Lord, you were with me and did guide me in the way. You feed me with the bread of Your sacraments. You clothe me with the wedding garment of charity. You have brought me to the mansion of glory which is Your home, O my Eternal Father. What remains, O Lord, but that I should protest that You are my God forever and ever. Amen.

We depend absolutely on our Saviour's redemption, who merited and suffered for us, who appeased the divine justice by loving obedience unto death, and the death on the cross which is the root of all the graces we receive: for we are the spiritual shoots engrafted on His stock. If being engrafted we remain in Him, we shall bear, by the life of grace He communicates to us, the fruits of glory He has prepared for us. If we are His by faith and works, He will be ours by glory. It is in our power to be His, for though it be a gift of God to be God's, it is a gift which God offers to all, and gives to those who consent to receive it.

He ardently desires we should be His, and He has proved Himself to be entirely ours, bestowing on us His death and His life: His life to save us from eternal death: His death to possess of eternal life. During its sojourn on earth, the soul who loves God remains in peace and serves God. To be His in this life and still more His in the next is all it desires. "O God", says St Augustine, "You have created my heart for Yourself, and it can never rest until it rests in You". "For what have I in heaven and besides You what do I desire on earth? You are the God of my heart, and the God that is my portion forever" (Ps. 72:25-6). The union to which our heart aspires cannot attain the fullness of its perfection in this mortal life; we can but commence our love on earth, to consummate it in heaven. The perfect union of the soul with God will be completed there, where the Lamb's marriage feast shall be made.

In heaven we shall be absorbed in God; the bond of love which unites our hearts to their sovereign principle will be eternal and indissoluble. But while we are here awaiting the kiss of union which we shall receive from the Spouse in glory, He gives us kisses and a thousand delicious feelings of His sacred presence, for unless the soul were embraced she would not be drawn, nor would she run in the odour of the Beloved's perfumes. "Let him kiss me with the kisses of his mouth" (Sg.1,1) for of all the kisses, of all the favours that my Spouse has given me, I only pant after the great and solemn marriage kiss which remains forever - which I shall receive when the veil is torn asunder and I meet my Beloved face to face.

Our Blessed Lady's Love of God

Our Blessed Lady! She is the daughter of divine love, the one only love, the all perfect spouse, our heavenly Queen. Her charity surpassed that of the seraphim, for "Many women have done admirable things, but you surpass them all!" (Prov.31,29). The charity of this mother of love excels in perfection that of all the saints in heaven. The Church considers that she never sinned venially. She never varied, nor did she tarry in the way of love, but advancing continually she ascended from love to love; so that love reigned peaceably in her soul and made all its acts at its pleasure. The purity of her heart and her virginity were more perfect than that of the angels, for her spirit was not divided. It could devote itself to the Lord's affairs, all it need worry about is "pleasing the Lord" (1 Cor.7,32) Her maternal love, that most wonderful, most active, most ardent of all love, what must it not have worked in the heart of such a mother and for the heart of such a Son! Her sleep was a sleep of love, since she never gave repose to her pure body but to reinvigorate it the better to serve her God.

She loved her virginal body not only because it was sweet, pure, humble, obedient to divine love, and wholly embalmed with love's sweetness, but also because it was the living source of our Saviour's and belonged entirely to Him. Well may we call her Tabernacle of Alliance, Ark of Sanctity, Throne of the Divinity. O Jesus, what were the dreams of Your most holy Mother? Were they not visions sweet and holy as she slept while her heart watched? Did she perhaps dream that she carried You once more in her womb? Or hanging at the sacred breasts or that You were again sweetly resting on those virginal lilies? Did she dream that as her divine Child once slept in her womb, that now she was sleeping in His pierced side, like a white dove in the cave of a rock? Was her sleep an ecstasy of love, while her body lay in sweet and grateful repose?

O Mother, Your heart remained perpetually inflamed with Your holy love which You received from Your Son; Your love could neither perish, diminish, nor remain in the same state: it never ceased to increase. You are the Mother of divine love - You will obtain for us the grace of love - You will set our hearts on fire with the love of God, for You are the Mother of fair love, the most amiable, the most loving, and the most beloved Mother of Your only Son Jesus Christ our Lord.

The Love of God and Humility

"Hold firmly to what you already have, and let nobody take your prize away from you" (Rev.3,11).

"Love is always patient and kind; it is never jealous; love is never boastful or conceited; it is never rude or selfish; it does not take offence, and is not resentful. Love takes no pleasure in other people's sins but delights in the truth; it is always ready to excuse, to trust, to hope, and to endure whatever comes" (1 Cor.13,4-7).

In this life our souls are never so full of the love of God that they may not lose it. In heaven the sweetness of God's beauty will occupy our understanding, and the delights of His goodness will wholly satiate our will. We shall no longer be subject to change for we shall be inseparably united to God.

Here, in the twilight, the soul has reason to fear lest she desert her Spouse to seek some other object which may engage her affections and deceive her. In heaven she will be with Him there, were He feeds and reposes in the mid-day. His light will be so clear and His sweetness will bind her so closely to Himself that she will no longer have the power or the will to forsake Him. But while we are on earth we are subject to changes of all kinds; we are liable to be bent on every side, to the right towards heavenly love, to the left towards earthly love.

Venial sin troubles charity. It holds it as a slave, hindering its freedom of action, and attaching us to creatures. It deprives us of the spiritual intimacy which should exist between God and the soul and we lose the interior helps which draw us to God. Those good for nothing souls who seek pleasure and whose hearts are set on transitory things may well fear that they no longer have charity, for they are in great danger of losing it. God allows us to be tried and tempted in this way, that in resisting we may exercise charity, that by fighting we may overcome ourselves, that being victorious we may triumph.

We are pilgrims in this life; most of us have voluntarily slept in sin, but God in His mercy touches our hearts and inflames them with His holy love. Ah! how it is that His love attracts so few and draws yet fewer? Those who listen to His voice and who follow His invitations have every reason to rejoice, but not to glorify themselves, because all they receive is from God, who leaves them the merit of their good works but reserves for Himself the glory thereof.

The love of men towards God takes its being, progress, and perfection from the eternal love of God towards men. All we are, all we have, we owe to God - of ourselves we are nothing - to Him alone is due all honour and all praise. "What do you have that was not given to you?" says the Apostle (1 Cor.4,7) We have received all from God, but especially the supernatural gifts of holy love. If we have any love for God, to Him is due the honour and glory who did all in us, without whom nothing is done, and as we are nothing, save by His grace, we ought to be nothing but for His glory. Would it not be vanity for such vile and abject creatures as we are to imagine that we are entitled to attribute to ourselves the glory of our conversion, just because we did not refuse to listen to the grace God gave us?

Let us love God with our whole hearts, and humbly adore His most holy will, thanking Him for all that He has done for us, and in us, saying, "Yahweh, what variety you have created, arranging everything so wisely!" (Ps.104,24) "Ordering all things for good" (Ws.8,1). If we are humble what have we to fear?

What ought we not to hope for, being the children of a Father so rich in goodness, who deigns to love us with an infinite love, and who wills to sanctify us and save us. He who is so clear-sighted to ordain, and so prudent to execute, bestows on us the fullness of His grace here in order to crown us with glory hereafter.

All things are from Him; all things are by Him; all things are in Him. To Him be all praise, all honour, and all glory, for ever and ever. Amen.

Informative Catholic Reading

We hope that you have enjoyed reading this booklet.

If you would like to find out more about CTS booklets - we'll send you our free information pack and catalogue.

Please send us your details:

Name ....

Address ....

....

....

Postcode ....

Telephone ....

Email ....

Send to: CTS, 40-46 Harleyford Road,
           Vauxhall, London
           SE11 5AY

Tel: 020 7640 0042
Fax: 020 7640 0046
Email: info@cts-online.org.uk